his ite

RAWN

17 WAYS TO SAVE THE WORLD

Louise Spilsbury and Mark Ruffle

W
FRANKLIN WATTS
LONDON • SYDNEY

CONTENTS

WHY DO WE NEED TO SAVE OUR WORLD?

Our world is unique. In the inky black vastness of space, Earth is the only planet we know where living things like us can survive. Other planets are giant balls of gas, icy wildernesses or endless and empty expanses of rock. Our world is full of water we can drink, air we can breathe and resources we can use.

Early humans drank from streams, gathered plants, hunted animals and lived a nomadic lifestyle. Gradually, people began to farm and settle down in villages and towns. With more food available, the human population increased. Together and over time, people built cities with roads, railways and airports, and developed machines to make life easier, from cars to computers. The bad news is that this amazing success story has come at a price, putting people, wildlife and the planet at risk.

Today, our wonderful world and all the people in it face some massive challenges. One of the biggest is inequality: some people have and use far more than they need, creating mountains of waste. Many others don't even get the water, food, electricity and other essentials they need to survive. Some people get chances and choices that many other people simply do not.

Inequality and the ways we use and overuse resources are causing some serious problems for the planet, too. Clean drinking water is not always available when and where people need it, and our actions are spoiling the soil, reducing the food we can grow. The fuels we burn create pollution and gases that make us ill and contribute to climate change. The climate crisis may be the biggest challenge of all as it also threatens to worsen the dangerous effects of extreme weather events such as floods, droughts and wildfires.

We have
reached a turning point
in the history of life on Earth and
it's time to take action. The United
Nations (UN) is an organisation set up to
help solve world problems and it represents
the people of 193 countries of the world.
On 25 September 2015, world leaders at the UN
adopted 17 Sustainable Development Goals (SDGs)
to help create a better world by 2030.

Sustainable development is about finding better ways of doing
things so we can improve the lives of everyone, everywhere,
while also protecting our world. The 17 SDGs aim to end poverty,
fight inequality and stop climate change; to help people, the
world's wildlife and the planet be safer and happier.

In this book we look at the big challenges the world
faces, their causes and how we can all take action
to address them through the SDGs. You may
have some great ideas of your
own already!

GOAL 1

No Poverty

Most people have enough money to buy all of the things they need and many of the things they want. However, some of the world's people live in poverty and don't have enough money for food, clean water, medicine, clothing, or a place to live that keeps them warm, dry and safe.

There are many causes of poverty and there are people living in poverty in every country. Poverty can happen when people lose their jobs or are paid too little for the jobs they do. It can happen when storms, floods or drought – events that are worsening and becoming more common with climate change – destroy homes and communities. In some places, war or conflict forces people to sell or leave behind all their belongings and flee from the land they relied on for food and work.

Many extremely poor people don't get the chance to go to school and that makes it much harder to get a job. People living in poverty are also more likely to get ill, which makes it harder to keep a job.

Once people are trapped in poverty, it's often very difficult for them to escape from it.

FACTS

Poverty hurts young people most. More than half of those living in extreme poverty are children.

A tenth of the world's population live in extreme poverty, surviving on less than US$1.90 a day.

Over half of the people living on less than $1.90 a day live in sub-Saharan Africa.

TAKE ACTION: GIVE

Since 1990, a billion people have risen out of extreme poverty, but there is still a long way to go to reach the goal of no poverty. Countries of the UN are tackling some of the root causes of poverty, for example creating jobs for poor people and improving access to schools, because with more education world poverty could be cut in half. You can help, too ...

Give up some time and write a letter to government officials, newspaper editors or local business leaders, about what causes child poverty and what we can do to end it.

Sharing is caring. When it's your birthday, suggest some friends or family give money to a charity that fights poverty instead of giving you a birthday gift.

Time for a spring clean! Sort out your cupboards and give unwanted clothes, books and toys to a charity shop that helps children in need.

Raise money to give to charities that provide help to people hit by famine or a natural disaster. Hold a talent show, art show, sponsored run, toy or bake sale and donate the proceeds.

GOAL 2

Zero Hunger

Hunger is more than a long wait for dinner or a rumbling stomach. Real hunger is when people become weak, tired and ill because they cannot buy, get or grow enough healthy food to eat week after week.

Poverty causes hunger when families cannot afford to buy food, or the land, tools and seeds they need to grow it. War causes hunger, too: people may be forced to abandon their farms, or bombs buried in fields make it unsafe for farmers to work. Extreme weather disasters, such as drought, floods and storms, destroy fields and crops, and some of the healthy soils we need to grow food are drying up and turning to dust as Earth's temperature rises.

Loading our plates with too much meat also causes problems. Growing crops, such as soya beans, to make feed for chickens, pigs and other animals uses vast amounts of farmland. If this land were used to grow plant proteins for people, we could feed far more of the world's population.

The other big issue is producing food that never gets eaten! Did you know that a third of all the food produced in the world goes to waste because it goes bad on the farm, gets lost or spoiled as it's transported or stored, or gets thrown away in shop, restaurant and home kitchens?

FACTS

About one in nine people in our world don't get enough food to be healthy and active.

More than four-fifths of the world's farmland is used to raise farm animals for meat.

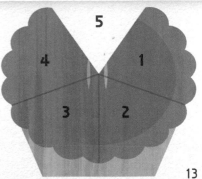

The world's population is growing and by 2050 there could be almost 10 billion people on the planet. We all need to eat, so what can we do to help make a world where there is zero hunger?

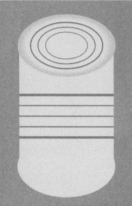

Donate tins or packets of food to a food bank.

Avoid food waste by making soup with leftovers or freezing them to eat later.

Monday

Tuesday

Wednesday

Thursday

Friday

Saturday

Sunday

Families can plan weekly menus before shopping so they don't buy food they don't need.

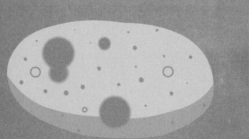

Store foods properly so they don't go rotten before there is time to cook or eat them.

Replace some meat meals with vegetarian ones and enjoy some plant proteins such as peas, beans and nuts instead. There will be more food to go around if we eat more plant crops ourselves, rather than feeding them to animals farmed for meat.

Shop at local farmers' markets. Food is usually fresher from a local market because it hasn't travelled so far.

14

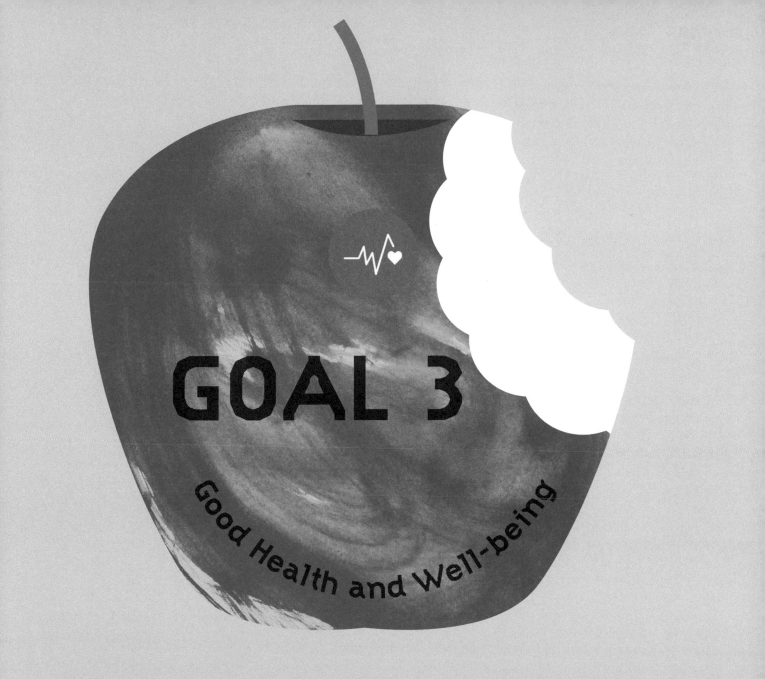

GOAL 3

Good Health and Well-being

Most people enjoy healthier lives today than they did in the past. Yet, some people still suffer from diseases that could be prevented, and more than 5 million children die each year before they've had a chance to celebrate their fifth birthday.

Many people simply cannot afford to buy the medicines and vaccines they need, or they live in the countryside and have no clinics or hospitals nearby. Even if they can get to a health centre, there may not be enough well-trained doctors or nurses to look after them properly or to give them the best advice about how to stay healthy.

People also die unnecessarily in road traffic accidents, from drinking dirty water because no clean water is available, breathing polluted air in congested cities, eating unhealthy diets, from smoking cigarettes or drinking too much alcohol.

+ More than half the people in the world don't have basic health services, such as a nearby clinic or doctor.

+ Over 7 million people die every year from breathing in polluted air.

+ More than 1.5 million people die from vaccine-preventable diseases each year.

+ Measles vaccinations saved the lives of around 20 million children between 2000 and 2016.

Most doctors say eating smaller portions of meat and dairy products, and more vegetables, seeds, pulses and nuts is so much healthier for people that it could save millions of lives a year, as well as being better for the planet, too!

Vegetables

Broccoli

Yam

Seeds

Sunflower

Chia

Pumpkin

Pulses

Chickpea

Black bean

Lentil

Nuts

Hazel

Pecan

Countries and charities are working to ensure healthy lives for all: trying to make medicines and vaccines affordable, reducing pollution and training more doctors. You can do your bit by living a healthy life and encouraging people you know to do the same.

Get vaccinated. Vaccinations prevent many diseases!

Work up a sweat! Find some sports or exercises you enjoy and do them regularly.

Eat good, wholesome and nutritious food.

Choose water, avoid sugary drinks and aim to eat five portions of vegetables and fruits a day.

Good mental health is as important as good physical health, so make time to relax, see friends and do things you enjoy.

Get a full night's sleep: for children aged 9–14, snoozing peacefully for 9 or 10 hours helps to keep your brain and body fighting fit!

Say no! Make healthy choices, like avoiding cigarettes.

QUALITY EDUCATION

Quality education matters. It gives people the knowledge and skills they need to stay healthy and it teaches them about the world and their rights. It helps them to get jobs, which helps their countries prosper, and when people learn about the world they are more likely to care about problems, such as climate change. Unfortunately, millions of children don't get the education they deserve.

For some children, the nearest school is simply too far away and they don't have transport to get there. Or they can't go because their family doesn't have enough money to pay the fees, or buy the uniform or books they need. Some children are kept away from school to work with their family or because people don't think they need an education since they are a girl or disabled. In war zones, bombs may destroy school buildings or force people to flee, leaving their schools behind.

Many children who make it to school still don't get a good education. Imagine how hard it is to learn when there aren't enough teachers or books to go around. What if the teachers aren't well trained, or when classrooms are noisy and overcrowded, or so full that lessons take place outdoors.

FACTS

Over 265 million children don't get the chance to go to school at all.

Over 600 million young people around the world lack basic maths and reading skills.

About half of children under 11 who are out of school live in places affected by war or conflict.

More than half of children not in school live in sub-Saharan Africa.

Sub-Saharan Africa

Countries of the UN are working towards providing free primary and secondary education for all, and making sure teachers have the spaces, training and materials they need to teach well. However there is still some way to go. Here's how you can help:

Do your best – make the most of your own education.

Learn about world education problems and talk about the issues with people you know.

Donate books to public libraries or schools in need.

Help others learn, such as a younger brother or sister who's struggling with a subject at school.

Spread learning: talk to teachers about sending books or computers to schools in need of them.

Get yourself a pen pal from another country and learn about each other's lives and cultures.

GOAL 5

Gender Equality

In the last hundred years, there have been huge improvements in gender equality, but many girls and women still do not get the same choices and chances as boys and men, and this is bad for all of us.

Gender equality is important for everyone, not just girls and women.

Around the world, more girls than boys are denied an education and many women don't have the chance to get a full-time job. Some girls are pressured into getting married when they are very young, or spend their time cleaning, caring for relatives or doing other unpaid chores at home.

Women in paid work have a smaller choice of jobs and often get paid less than men. Women and girls are also more likely to experience violence and cruelty and less likely to get the healthcare they need.

Gender equality
gives boys and men,
as well as girls and women,
more freedom to step outside
stereotypes and be themselves.
Equal work and pay for women
means whole families and countries
are better off. The more women who
get the chance to succeed in work
and politics, the more talent and
ideas we will have to tackle
planet problems, such as
climate change.

Less than a fifth of government ministers and fewer than 25 world leaders are women.

Globally, women are paid about 25 per cent less than men. This is known as the gender wage gap.

Of all the people in the world who haven't been taught to read, two-thirds are women.

TAKE ACTION: EMPOWER

UN countries are working to ensure girls and women get equal education and training, healthcare, decent work and fair pay, and more of a voice in making decisions and choices that affect the world. Girls and boys have a role to play in achieving gender equality, too.

+ Share chores evenly in the home – don't fall into stereotypes of boys cleaning the cars and girls doing the dishes – these are both useful skills for everyone.

+ Empower others – talk about gender equality and how important it is and call out examples of when it does not happen at home, school, on the street or in the media.

+ Empower yourself: be true to your feelings and not how society expects you to behave according to your gender. Boys should not be afraid to cry and be gentle, and girls should not be afraid to be strong and opinionated.

+ You can be anything you want to be, regardless of your gender. Encourage people to follow their dreams and skills, and to ignore people who try to tell them otherwise.

GOAL 6
Clean Water and Sanitation

GOAL 6   CLEAN WATER AND SANITATION

Clean, fresh water is one of the world's most precious resources, but only 1 per cent of the world's water is drinkable – the rest is salty seawater or frozen in polar ice caps and glaciers. This amount has to be shared by every living thing on Earth and billions of people don't have the water they need to drink, grow food and cook with, or to stay clean and healthy.

When clean water and sanitation are in short supply, people suffer. Diseases that spread because of dirty or germ-filled water or a lack of sinks and toilets are the main cause of death for children under five. People go hungry when farmers struggle to get the water they need for crops and farm animals. Without a water supply near home, women and children spend hours walking to wells to collect back-breaking loads of water instead of working, going to school or caring for their families.

There are several reasons for this water crisis. There are more people on the planet than ever before, and people pollute and waste a lot of water. Farms and factories use vast amounts of water to grow and make things, and some industries spoil water supplies by releasing dirt and waste into them. Fresh water is also wasted by leaky pipes and polluted by waste rotting in landfills. Climate change is a culprit, too, causing dry spells in some places and dangerous floods in others, which destroy useful water supplies by washing dirt and debris into them.

FACTS

✖ Three in ten people don't have safe drinking water and about 3 billion people don't have a toilet to use.

✖ The majority of the world's dirty drain water is flushed straight into rivers and seas.

✖ Eight hundred children die every day from diseases linked to or caused by unsafe water.

TAKE ACTION: CONSERVE

Countries of the UN are working to protect water supplies, help villages build wells and toilets and teach everyone the importance of hygiene habits, such as hand-washing. One way we can all help is by conserving water and wasting less.

Get your school to fundraise for people who live without safe water on World Water Day and World Toilet Day.

Be alert about leaks: a leaky tap can waste thousands of litres of water every year.

Use a bucket instead of a hose when you're helping to wash the car.

Save water when you flush the toilet by using the smaller button or lifting the handle up once waste is washed away.

Turn off the tap while cleaning your teeth and take shorter showers.

Take care what you throw down sinks and toilets: paints, oils, medicines or other litter cause pollution that is costly to clean up and damaging to rivers and lakes.

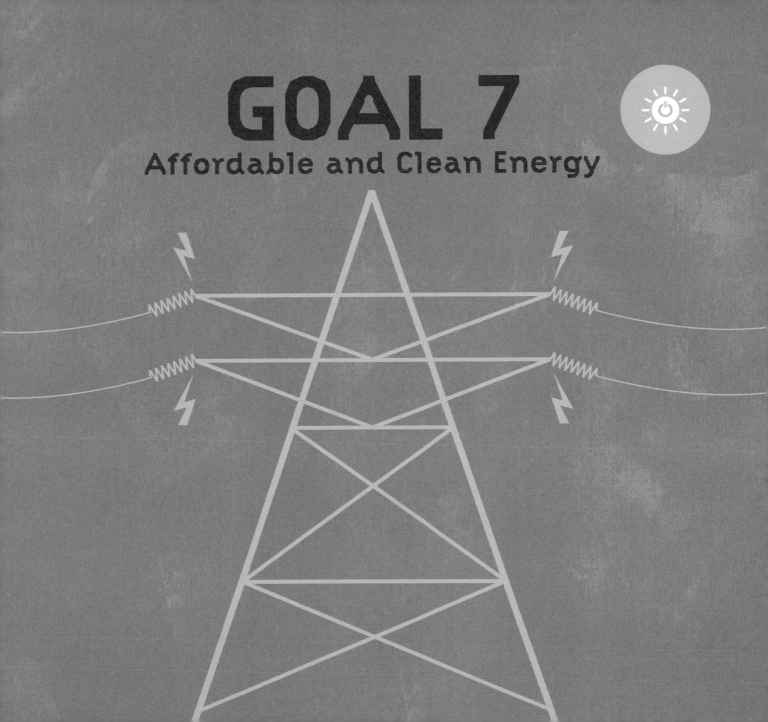

GOAL 7

Affordable and Clean Energy

GOAL 7 ☀ AFFORDABLE AND CLEAN ENERGY

Many of us flick a switch to turn on a light or computer without a thought for how electricity is made, what life would be like without it or how much we use. Power is a problem. Almost one billion people in the world can't afford or get the electricity they need to improve their lives. We need to make more of it, but currently most is made in unsustainable ways that harm people and the planet.

Without electricity, doctors have to do life-saving operations by candlelight and have no fridges to store vaccines. It is difficult to run a successful business and schoolchildren struggle to do homework at night. People cook or heat homes with fuels like charcoal and coal, which cause indoor air pollution and ill-health.

Access to electricity can change lives, but there are downsides to power stations that burn coal, natural gas and oil to make electricity. Not only are these fossil fuels limited resources that will run out one day, but burning them releases dirty particles and carbon dioxide gas. Air pollution causes breathing problems, makes people ill and can even kill. Carbon dioxide is one of the so-called greenhouse gases that traps heat in Earth's atmosphere, causing climate change.

We must make sure everyone has access to clean, reliable energy!

FACTS

✖ Around 3 billion people rely on wood, coal, charcoal or animal dung for cooking and heating, resulting in over 4 million deaths each year from indoor air pollution.

✖ Energy accounts for around 60 per cent of total global greenhouse gas emissions.

GOAL 7

TAKE ACTION: SAVE

The UN is encouraging countries to reduce fossil fuel use and increase their use of clean, renewable energies, such as wind farms and hydropower plants. These turn energy from flowing wind or water into electricity without releasing pollution and greenhouse gases. How can you support this change?

Wear an extra sweater instead of turning the heating up when you're chilly.

Open a window instead of turning on a fan or the air conditioning when you're hot.

Use a lid when boiling water in a pan. This saves energy and makes the water boil more quickly.

Get your family to choose fridges and other appliances that use less energy.

Change to energy-efficient LED bulbs in all household lights and lamps.

Encourage your family to switch to a green energy supplier or talk to your school about getting solar power.

Wash clothes at lower temperatures in washing machines and dry them outdoors rather than in a power-hungry tumble drier.

34

GOAL 8

Decent Work and Economic Growth

1

It feels good to have regular, satisfying work and to earn a fair wage so you can help to take care of yourself and your family. Unfortunately, an estimated 172 million people are without work, and many people who are in work are poorly paid. Decent work is important because it helps families lift themselves out of poverty and improves a country's wealth, health and happiness.

In some places, the problem is that there simply aren't enough jobs to go around. In others, people struggle to find a career because they haven't had education or training to give them the skills they need. Discrimination is a factor, too. That's when an employer unfairly refuses a job to someone who is perfectly able to do it because of who they are; women, people of different ethnicities and disabled people are often discriminated against.

Some people can't start up or expand small businesses that could create more jobs because they don't have access to banks to get loans to help them grow.

Many people who do have jobs are not paid a fair wage. Some are paid so little they are slaves in all but name. Others have no job security: they don't work regular hours so don't know how much they will earn or live in fear that they could be sacked at any time without warning. Some workers are shouted at or even beaten. Others may work for 14-hour days with few breaks, even to go to the toilet. Some workers may not be allowed holidays or time off work. Others work in unsafe or unhealthy conditions where there is a real risk of injury or long-term health problems.

GOAL 8

TAKE ACTION: PROMOTE

The UN is not only promoting the spread of decent work, but also the creation of new jobs that will help to restore and protect the environment and natural resources. For example, training local people as guides to show tourists the importance of protecting rainforests. We can all help to promote decent work and economic growth, too.

+ Buy products with the Fairtrade logo showing they were made in decent working conditions, by people who are paid well and in a sustainable way.

+ Encourage your school to stock fair trade goods, too.

+ Avoid buying lots of very cheap stuff: these are more likely to have been made in an unfair and unsustainable way.

+ If you see a post about workers' rights or sustainable products, share it so people in your network see it too.

+ Learn about workers' rights: knowing what people are entitled to helps people improve their lives.

GOAL 9

Industry, Innovation and Infrastructure

INDUSTRY, INNOVATION AND INFRASTRUCTURE

Imagine that you have to go to work, but there are no roads to get you there. Or you have a rural business making clothes, but there are no cargo trains to deliver them to the city. Infrastructure – such as roads and bridges, phones and Internet, water reservoirs and electricity cables – is vital for empowering communities, but there is a big gap in the development of infrastructure globally.

Without basic infrastructure, it is difficult for people in many developing countries to go to school, work, or markets to buy and sell goods, so they struggle to get an education, a better job and better wages. When people have to walk long distances to get basic services, it costs them time and money and makes it harder for them to escape poverty.

Without mobile masts or Internet access, small businesses cannot contact suppliers and customers or find the best places to sell their products.

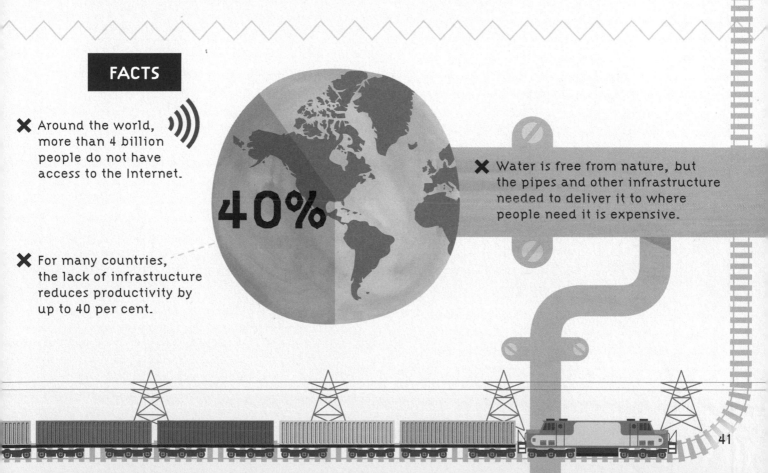

The world faces a big challenge: developing countries need new infrastructure to prosper, but often rely on old-style infrastructure, such as fossil fuel power stations and fuel-guzzling cars and lorries belching out polluting gases. This is harming the planet. We need smart new technologies and innovations to create sustainable infrastructure that uses resources and energy more efficiently.

FACTS

✖ Around the world, more than 4 billion people do not have access to the Internet.

40%

✖ For many countries, the lack of infrastructure reduces productivity by up to 40 per cent.

✖ Water is free from nature, but the pipes and other infrastructure needed to deliver it to where people need it is expensive.

TAKE ACTION: CHOOSE

Among other things, the UN is spreading the word about the importance of sustainable infrastructure around the world and encouraging banks and businesses to invest in new high-tech products. There are lots of ways we can all choose to help, too.

 Buy from local producers and businesses who advertise their sustainable practices.

 Click! If you need to shop online, choose smaller online businesses that are making an effort to be more sustainable.

 Choose to donate old, working mobile phones to a charity so someone else can use them.

 Create a hotspot map to show people where there are public spaces with free WiFi access to enable more people to use the Internet.

 Choose an exciting 'green career' in the future and work to help solve global challenges. You could get a job designing energy-efficient buildings, engineering electric cars and planes, or even new ways to generate power without fossil fuels.

GOAL 10
Reduced Inequalities

Villages without electricity, people without jobs, children without teachers, clinics without vaccines ... these are all examples of inequality. Over the past 25 years, inequality between people has increased, causing harm around the world.

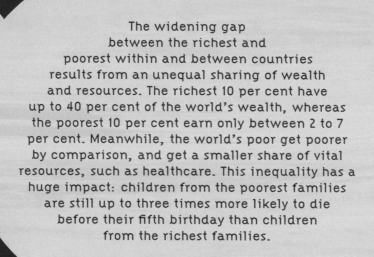

The widening gap between the richest and poorest within and between countries results from an unequal sharing of wealth and resources. The richest 10 per cent have up to 40 per cent of the world's wealth, whereas the poorest 10 per cent earn only between 2 to 7 per cent. Meanwhile, the world's poor get poorer by comparison, and get a smaller share of vital resources, such as healthcare. This inequality has a huge impact: children from the poorest families are still up to three times more likely to die before their fifth birthday than children from the richest families.

Another kind of inequality is caused by prejudice. Some people are told they cannot live in certain places, do certain jobs or earn as much as others because of their sex, gender, race or religion, because they have a disability or because they are refugees in a new country. They may be ignored, badly treated, insulted, hurt or even killed because of this unfair and unjust discrimination.

Reducing inequality is vital for helping people and the planet prosper.

FACTS

✗ People from poor communities can expect to die 10 to 20 years earlier than people in wealthy areas.

♀ Women in rural areas are three times more likely to die while giving birth than women in cities.

♿ People who have disabilities are up to five times more likely than average to struggle to buy essentials, such as food and clothing, as a direct result of having to pay for healthcare.

Many countries in the UN are working to reduce inequality, for example by making laws to stop people being treated unfairly and ensuring everyone can vote in elections and choose changes to improve their lives. You can oppose inequality, too; raise your voice against discrimination and stick up for people who aren't being treated fairly.

If you see someone being bullied, treated badly or unfairly because of prejudice, you could check that they're OK and tell a teacher or other adult.

If you notice harassment on an online message board or in a chat room, tell the administrator for that site.

Oppose ignorance by suggesting or arranging a world culture day at school to help other students understand prejudice and oppose inequality.

If someone new comes to school, such as a refugee from another country, make the effort to welcome the student and help them settle in and get to know people.

Oppose hate with kindness. Treat everyone with kindness and respect and appreciate all of our similarities and differences.

GOAL 11

Sustainable Cities and Communities

Half of Earth's population live in cities and more and more of us flock to big, bustling urban centres every year. At their best, cities are hubs for ideas, business, science and culture that help people and the planet. At their worst, cities cause serious problems for both.

The average city dweller, especially in wealthy, developed countries, tends to buy more stuff and make more waste than the average person in the countryside. City dwellers use more electricity and choke city roads with slow-moving cars, polluting the air with dirty exhaust fumes. In fact, although cities only cover 3 per cent of Earth's land, they are responsible for up to 80 per cent of the world's energy use and 70 per cent of its carbon emissions!

Cities can be bad for people as well as the planet. 9 out of 10 urban residents breathe unsafe, polluted air and since 2016, over 4 million have died as a result. Waste piled in city streets when there is a lack of refuse trucks and landfill sites can become a breeding ground for disease. A shortage of decent housing leaves many people living in overcrowded and unsafe slums without sufficient clean water and toilets, and where diseases can spread easily.

FACTS

✗ By 2030, 5 billion people are likely to be living in cities.

✗ Over 1 billion people live in slums and this number is rising.

✗ Two billion people do not have waste collection services.

We need to build smart cities where people can go about their daily lives without harming the environment. For example with sustainable public transport instead of cars and buildings covered in plants to reduce noise and air pollution. There are things you can do, too.

+ Go for it! Bike or walk when you can to get fit and save fuel.

+ Go by bus, train or other public transport instead of by car when you can.

+ Never drop litter – go and find a bin or take it home and put it in your dustbin there.

+ Go out of your way to help take care of parks and other public spaces. You could water plants at a playground or join a community litter clean-up.

+ Shop, eat and drink locally. Supporting neighbourhood businesses keeps people employed and circulates money back into your community.

+ Value your city and celebrate its history and culture by visiting and learning about its old buildings and traditions.

50

More, more, more ... The more we buy, or consume, the more stuff factories and companies make, or produce. This cycle of consumption and production is spinning out of control and harming us and our precious planet.

It takes a lot of natural resources to make stuff: soil and water to grow plants for food and fabric, trees to make wood and paper, oil to make plastic, minerals to make everything from steel to the electronics in mobile phones, and so on. Some resources are being used up so quickly that they are in danger of running out.

Getting natural resources, such as metals, out of the ground can also damage habitats and the environment. The machines that do this work use fossil fuels, creating more pollution and greenhouse gases that contribute to climate change.

It takes a lot of fuel to transport those raw materials to factories. In turn, factories use lots of electricity to make them into products. Then, yet more fuel is used to carry the products to the shops where we buy them. The more stuff we buy, the more we throw away in landfills or burn in incinerators. As waste rots or burns, it causes more problems by releasing pollution into the land and more heat-trapping gases into the air!

FACTS

The fashion industry uses 93 billion cubic metres of water every year. That's enough for 5 million people to survive. It takes 10,000 litres of water to make a single pair of jeans.

If the world's population reaches almost 10 billion by 2050, as expected, and people make and buy as much stuff as they do today, we will need the equivalent of almost three planets to provide the natural resources to produce it.

53

∞ **TAKE ACTION: REUSE**

The UN is encouraging people to find ways to use natural resources carefully, for example by buying less and reducing waste so there are enough resources for everyone to share in the future. Reusing stuff is one way we can all do more and do better with less!

+ Reuse as much as possible. Instead of buying new clothes, mend, patch or dye old ones.

+ Reuse books from public libraries or swap your own with friends.

+ Buy second-hand items from shops or online, so even if someone else isn't going to reuse it, you can.

+ Come up with creative ways of reusing shoe boxes, butter tubs and other containers to store things or for arts and crafts.

+ Get broken machines repaired in a workshop instead of dumping them and buying new.

+ Only buy things you really need. Reducing the amount you buy, reduces how much you throw away too.

GOAL 13

Climate Action

The fact that Earth's temperature has risen by about 1°C in the last 140 years may not sound like much, but if we get a fever, a 1°C rise makes us feel too hot, ill and tired. Climate change is making Earth sick, too: it's having dramatic and dangerous effects on people, wildlife and the planet.

Our planet is surrounded by a blanket of gases that helps trap heat from the Sun and keeps Earth warm enough to live on. Human activities are adding more carbon dioxide and other greenhouse gases to the atmosphere, trapping more heat and increasing Earth's average temperatures.

Greenhouse gases are released when large amounts of fossil fuel are burned to power machines, homes, factories and vehicles. They are also produced when waste rots and when cows and other farm animals release gas. When forests are burned or cut down and left to rot on the forest floor, the carbon stored inside the trees is released into the atmosphere as carbon dioxide, too.

Warmer temperatures upset Earth's natural balance. Ice at the poles is melting, causing sea levels to rise and threatening to drown low-lying coastlines and islands. Warming ocean water harms ocean wildlife, such as coral. Long dry periods of drought kill crops and threaten food supplies and heatwaves cause ferocious wildfires that rampage for weeks. Warmer temperatures also increase the chances of extreme and destructive weather events, such as hurricane-force winds and heavy floods.

FACTS

✗ Today the concentration of carbon dioxide, or CO_2, in the atmosphere is almost 50 per cent higher than before the Industrial Revolution (1760–1840).

✗ Sea levels have risen by about 20 cm since 1880 and are expected to rise another 30–122 cm by 2100.

✗ To limit global warming to 1.5 °C, CO_2 emissions must drop by 45 per cent between 2010 and 2030.

The UN is helping countries and businesses take action in a variety of ways, from designing vehicles that burn less fuel to charging polluting companies a carbon tax if they cause unnecessary emissions. You can make a change, too:

 Encourage your family to take trains not planes for holidays and enjoy the view from your window as you travel.

 Write a letter to your local or school newspaper about climate change. The more people talk about the issue, the better!

 Write letters to local and national governments asking what action they are taking to fight climate change.

 Stop appliances sucking up energy when turned off by unplugging phone and laptop chargers when not in use and using power strips for lights and TVs.

 Consider reducing the amount of meat you eat and buy meat from local farmers to cut food-related greenhouse gas emissions.

 Try to eat mostly in-season and locally grown fruits and vegetables to cut down on the energy used to grow and transport food.

GOAL 14

Life Below Water

Oceans teem with life. Seahorses, starfish, sharks and other amazing creatures feed, swim and have their young in this beautiful blue world.

People depend on oceans, too. Tiny ocean plants release half of all the oxygen we need to breathe. Ocean waters soak up carbon dioxide from the air, helping to slow our planet's climate change. On top of all of this, billions of people rely on oceans for transport, food, jobs and for fun.

Tiny ocean plants

Oceans look after us, but we are not taking such good care of the oceans. We take too many fish out of the sea before they have had the chance to produce their young. This reduces fish numbers, so there are fewer for sea creatures – and us – to eat.

One of the biggest threats to our oceans is plastic waste.

Sea turtles choke on plastic bags they mistake for jellyfish, seabirds feed their chicks with tiny plastic bits instead of food, old fishing nets strangle seals and other animals, and plastic waste damages coral reefs that shelter millions of animals.

FACTS

One in two turtles have eaten plastic.

Nine out of ten seabirds have plastic blocking up their stomachs.

About 8 million tons of plastic – enough to cover every centimetre of coastline in the world – gets into the oceans each year.

By 2050, there could be more plastic in the oceans than fish.

Half of all the plastic stuff we buy is only used once. When we throw it away, it can end up in the oceans. Wind blows plastic bags off landfill sites. Rain washes plastic litter off streets. People flush plastic waste down sewage systems; this plastic gets into drains that carry waste into rivers that flow into oceans.

You can help save the oceans by preventing plastic waste.

✗ Glitter is made from tiny bits of plastic. Add sparkle to your pictures using alternatives instead.

✗ Plastic straws suck. Sip your drink from a glass or use a reusable bamboo or steel straw instead.

➕ Switch to reusable bottles and cups rather than buying drinks in disposable ones.

➕ Store your packed lunch in reusable containers and waxed cloth instead of plastic bags and clingfilm.

➕ Carry shopping in reusable bags instead of throwaway plastic ones.

➕ Buy items that are not made of plastic or that are made from recycled plastic.

➕ If you live near the coast, join a beach clean-up and help pick up seaside litter.

62

GOAL 15
Life on Land

GOAL 15   LIFE ON LAND

Life on land is remarkable. The land filters our water and helps us grow food, build homes, produce energy and transport goods. Without land and the plants and animals on it we would not be able to eat, breathe or live. So, why are we treating the land like dirt?

Forests cover almost a third of our planet's land. Trees help fight climate change and help animals breathe by absorbing carbon dioxide and producing oxygen. Trees provide people with food, medicines and jobs. Yet, people are cutting and burning vast areas of these leafy wonders for timber, fuel, or to clear land for farms, cities, roads or mines.

When trees are gone, there are no roots to hold soil and trap water, no fallen leaves to rot and replenish nutrients, and no branches to create shade. Unprotected soil dries out and blows away, leaving degraded land where little can grow. Plants also die and soils dry out as climate change causes longer or more frequent droughts.

Mistreating the land threatens wildlife as well as people. Forests are home to 80 per cent of land plants and animals. When their habitats are damaged, animals have nowhere to live, feed or raise their young. As a result, some become extinct. Crimes, such as poaching elephants for ivory tusks and tigers for their skins and bones, makes it even harder to protect our planet's precious wildlife.

FACTS

✘ The equivalent of about 27 football fields-worth of forest are destroyed every minute.

✘ About one fifth of Earth's land is being degraded and this is affecting the lives of 1 billion people.

✘ Almost a quarter of all animal species we know about are at risk of extinction.

Up to a hundred animal species are lost each day as a result of habitat destruction.

GOAL 15

TAKE ACTION: PROTECT

With the UN's help, countries are working to protect and restore land and forests, for example by making laws to stop poaching and pollution, or creating nature reserves where land and wildlife are protected. You can help protect life on land, too.

Plant a tree!

Buy paper and products with the FSC logo: this guarantees they are made from trees grown in forests that are replanted after being harvested, or allowed to regrow naturally.

Leave wild areas in your garden or put up a bird box to help local wildlife.

Organise or join a park or forest clean-up.

Go for a walk or visit a local wood or park. The more natural spaces are used, the more people will care for them.

Recycle paper, glass, plastic, metal and old electronics to reduce the amount of minerals and other raw materials taken from land (and waste generated) when producing new stuff.

Compost food scraps to reduce waste and recycle nutrients back into soils.

GOAL 16

Peace, Justice and Strong Institutions

Most people take it for granted that they live in peace and safety, going about their lives free from fear or harm. Many people around the world face a different, far harsher reality: they suffer horrific brutality and abuse or live with a dark cloud of violence hanging over them every day.

Many people are killed or sustain life-changing injuries as a result of war, crime, or corrupt governments, but violence ruins lives in other ways, too. It stops countries prospering and robs people of their chance to be happy or successful: did you know that over 28 million children under 11 cannot go to school because of conflict?

Men, women and many children are also tricked or violently forced from home and taken elsewhere to become modern-day slaves. Victims of this human trafficking are forced to work for no pay in homes, farms, factories or on the streets, and are often cruelly treated, beaten and starved.

Violence and crime happen when there are no laws to protect people or laws are not fairly enforced. This may be because criminals bribe police officers, lawyers and judges to let them get away with serious crimes or to avoid paying taxes. This means people are unprotected and there is less money to build the strong institutions that could give them the peace and justice they deserve.

FACTS

Half of the children in the world experience violence every year.

Every 5 minutes, somewhere in the world, a child is killed by violence.

Almost 26 million people — half of them children — are refugees who left their homelands to escape violence and persecution.

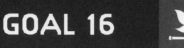
One of the many things the UN is doing to bring peace and justice to all is ensuring that everyone has identity documents. For example, a birth certificate proving how old and who someone is can help protect vulnerable people from crimes, such as human trafficking. You can work for peace and justice, too.

Show you care by writing to politicians to ask what they are doing to stop violence and abuse.

Stand up for what's right — if you see something that is unfair, speak up about it.

Support caring charities that work to stop human trafficking.

Know your rights: to access justice, knowing what you are entitled to goes a long way.

Vote! Take advantage of your right to elect leaders in your school council.

Avoid violence at all costs. Sort out arguments by listening to other people's point of view and talking things through calmly to find a shared solution and help others to do the same.

The challenges facing our world seem so big and difficult they can make us feel scared and powerless, but we're not. People can be extremely powerful when they join forces and even small actions can make a big difference if everyone, everywhere works together.

In today's world, we are all interconnected. Everything is connected to everything else. Problems and challenges, such as poverty and climate change, are never just confined to one country or region. Like plastic in the ocean or pollution in the air, problems drift and flow around the world, impacting all of us in one way or another.

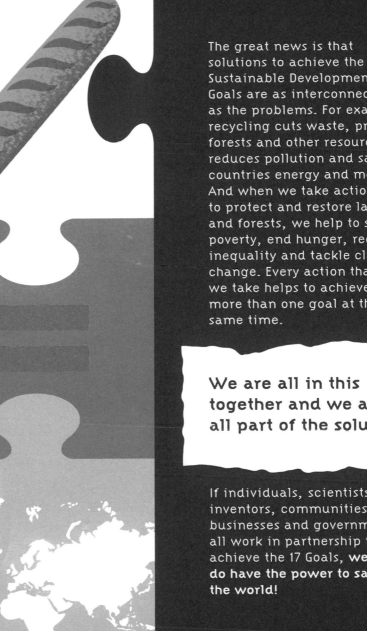

The great news is that solutions to achieve the Sustainable Development Goals are as interconnected as the problems. For example, recycling cuts waste, protects forests and other resources, reduces pollution and saves countries energy and money. And when we take action to protect and restore land and forests, we help to solve poverty, end hunger, reduce inequality and tackle climate change. Every action that we take helps to achieve more than one goal at the same time.

We are all in this together and we are all part of the solution.

If individuals, scientists, inventors, communities, businesses and governments all work in partnership to achieve the 17 Goals, **we do have the power to save the world!**

GOAL 17

 TAKE
ACTION: **UNITE**

The UN is helping countries and governments share knowledge, skills, ideas and technology to help each other achieve the 17 Sustainable Development Goals. We all need to unite to make the difference.

+ Tell everyone you know about the 17 Goals. People are more likely to listen to friends or family than experts and are more willing to act when it's important to someone they know.

+ Join in local events such as sports days and festivals to get to know others in your community.

+ Come up with creative new ways to explain the urgency of taking action to people.

+ Work with others as a team whenever you get the chance, in sports teams, by volunteering and by sharing household chores among all family members, for example.

+ Write letters to local community, business and government leaders to ask what they are doing and how you can help.

FURTHER INFORMATION

The UN's educational resources about the 17 Sustainable Development Goals are at:
www.un.org/sustainabledevelopment/student-resources

Find out more about each Sustainable Development Goal using this part of the UN website:
www.un.org/sustainabledevelopment/sustainable-development-goals

Looking for books that support the aims of the Sustainable Development Goals? The UN have a Sustainable Development Goals Book Club at:
www.un.org/sustainabledevelopment/sdgbookclub

Review all 17 of the SDGs by watching this UN video:
www.youtube.com/watch?v=0XTBYMfZyrM

Download a poster from the Royal Geographical Society showing the 17 Sustainable Development Goals:
www.rgs.org/schools/teaching-resources/the-sustainable-development-goals-infographic

THE SUSTAINABLE DEVELOPMENT GOALS
THE GOALS TO TRANSFORM OUR WORLD

 End poverty in all its forms everywhere.

 End hunger, achieve improved nutrition and promote sustainable agriculture.

 Ensure healthy lives and promote well-being.

 Ensure inclusive and quality education for all and promote lifelong learning opportunities.

 Achieve gender equality and empower all women and girls.

 Ensure availability and sustainable management of water and sanitation for all.

 Ensure access to affordable, reliable, sustainable and modern energy for all.

 Promote inclusive and sustainable economic growth, and decent work for all.

 Build strong infrastructure, promote inclusive and sustainable industry, and encourage innovation.

 Reduce inequality within and among countries.

 Make cities and human settlements inclusive, safe, strong and sustainable.

 Ensure sustainable consumption and production systems.

 Take urgent action to combat climate change and its impacts.

 Conserve and sustainably use the oceans, seas and marine resources.

 Protect, restore and promote sustainable use of ecosystems, stop and reverse habitat destruction, and stop biodiversity loss.

 Promote peaceful and inclusive societies, provide access to justice for all, and build effective, responsible and inclusive institutions.

 Strengthen the means of carrying out and revitalise the global partnership for sustainable development.

GLOSSARY

atmosphere blanket of gases that surrounds planet Earth

carbon dioxide greenhouse gas released when fossil fuels are burned and plants respire

climate change long-term shift in Earth's weather patterns and average temperatures

culture the beliefs, values and ways of behaving and celebrating that a particular group of people share

developed country a country with a lot of industries and factories and where people generally have high incomes

developing country a country with few industries and factories and where people generally have low incomes

discrimination treating one person or group of people less fairly or less well than other people or groups

drought long period of time with little or no rain

economic growth the increase in what a country produces and earns over time

emission the release of a substance, such as gas or heat, into the atmosphere

energy power or electricity needed in order to make things, such as computers, work

environment the natural world

extinction when a plant or animal species dies out

fair trade when producers in developing countries are paid a fair price for their work by companies in developed countries

famine when there is not access to enough food for a large number of people

fertiliser substance that helps plants grow bigger or better

flood an overflow of a large amount of water over what is normally dry land

fossil fuels fuels, such as coal, oil or natural gas, that are formed from the remains of plants and animals that died millions of years ago

glacier a very slow-moving river of ice

global warming gradual warming of the Earth's surface as a result of more greenhouse gases being trapped in Earth's atmosphere

greenhouse gas gas in Earth's atmosphere that traps heat from the Sun on Earth. Some exist naturally; others are released into the air by burning fuels, such as coal or oil

habitat place where plants and animals live

heatwave periods of time when an area experiences unusually high temperatures

incinerator giant oven that burns waste and turns it to ash

Industrial Revolution the time during which work began to be done more by machines in factories than by hand (1760–1840)

infrastructure facilities a country has to make it work, such as roads, railways, roads, bridges and airports

institution a large and important organisation, such as a police force

landfill a large hole in the ground where rubbish is buried

minerals solid substances that make up the rocks of our planet

nature reserve area of land that is protected in order to keep safe the animals and plants that live there

nomadic moving from one place to another rather than living in one place

nutrients substances that living things need to help them live and grow

poaching illegally catching or killing animals

pollution substance that makes air, soil or water unclean or unsafe to use

prejudice ideas or opinions about a person or group simply because they belong to a particular race, religion or other group

protein nutrient found in food that is essential for building, maintaining and repairing body cells

rainforest thick forest of tall trees found in tropical areas where there is a lot of rain

refugee a person forced to flee their homeland because of war or persecution

renewable energy a type of energy that comes from sources that don't use up natural resources or harm the environment, such as wind or the sun

resource something that is useful to people, such as water or soil

rights basic freedoms and protections everyone should have

rural to do with or found in the countryside

sanitation the systems for taking dirty water and other waste away from buildings in order to protect people's health

sea level the average height of the sea where it meets the land

species a group of living things that have similar characteristics and are capable of breeding

tax money paid to governments so that they can pay for public services, such as waste disposal

timber wood used for building and furniture

vaccine a substance that helps protect against certain diseases

wildfire a large, destructive fire that spreads quickly through trees and other plants

INDEX

Franklin Watts
First publishied in Great Britain in 2020 by the Watts Publishing Group

HB ISBN: 978 1 4451 7107 4
eBook ISBN: 978 1 4451 7347 4

Author: Louise Spilsbury
Design and Artwork: Mark Ruffle
Publisher: Paul Rockett
Managing Editor: John Hort
Production Controller: Inka Roszkowska

Franklin Watts
An imprint of Hachette Children's Group
Part of the Watts Publishing Group
Carmelite House
50 Victoria Embankment
London EC4Y 0DZ

An Hachette UK Company
www.hachette.co.uk

Printed in Dubai

FSC MIX Paper from responsible sources FSC® C104740
www.fsc.org